The National Poetry Series was established in _____ the publi-
cation of five poetry books annually through five participating publish-
ers. Publication is funded by the Lannan Foundation; Stephen Graham;
Joyce & Seward Johnson Foundation; Glenn and Renee Schaeffer,
Juliet Lea Hillman Simonds Foundation; and Charles B. Wright III.

**NATIONAL
ENDOWMENT
FOR THE ARTS**

2008 COMPETITION WINNERS

Anna Journey of Houston, Texas, *If Birds Gather Your Hair for Nesting*
Chosen by Thomas Lux, University of Georgia Press

Douglas Kearney of Van Nuys, California, *The Black Automaton*
Chosen by Catherine Wagner, Fence Books

Adrian Matejka of Edwardsville, Illinois, *Mixology*
Chosen by Kevin Young, Penguin Books

Kristin Naca of Minneapolis, Minnesota, *Bird Eating Bird*
Chosen by Yusef Komunyakaa for The National Poetry Series mtvU Prize,
HarperCollins Publishers

Sarah O'Brien of Brookfield, Ohio, *Catch Light*
Chosen by David Shapiro, Coffee House Press

catch light

POEMS

Sarah O'Brien

COFFEE HOUSE PRESS
MINNEAPOLIS
2009

Coffee House Press books are available to the trade through our primary distributor, Consortium Book Sales & Distribution, www.cbsd.com or (800) 283-3572. For personal orders, catalogs, or other information, write to: info@coffeehousepress.org.

Coffee House Press is a nonprofit literary publishing house. Support from private foundations, corporate giving programs, government programs, and generous individuals helps make the publication of our books possible. We gratefully acknowledge their support in detail in the back of this book.

Good books are brewing at coffeehousepress.org

LIBRARY OF CONGRESS CATALOGING-IN-PUBLICATION DATA
O'Brien, Sarah Frances.
Catch light : poems / by Sarah O'Brien.
p. cm.
ISBN 978-1-56689-237-7 (alk. paper)
I. Title.
PS3615.B7785C38 2009
811'.6—DC22
2009020906
FIRST EDITION | FIRST PRINTING
1 3 5 7 9 8 6 4 2
PRINTED IN THE UNITED STATES

ACKNOWLEDGMENTS
The author would like to heartily thank the editors of *Columbia: A Journal of Literature and Art*, *eleven/eleven*, *The Laurel Review*, and *Thermos*, where some of these poems first appeared.

I would also like to thank all of my friends who commented on and encouraged this manuscript; thank you, dear workshop-mates. I owe an especially fervent thanks to Cole Swensen for her unwavering support and unfaltering enthusiasm. Thank you David Shapiro, you made my year. Thanks Mom & Dad. And of course—Deon, thank you a thousand times.

for Deon Kay

CONTENTS

CAPTIONS

FIVE EYES

CLOUD & BULB

FINALLY A PHOTOGRAPH

A MANUAL OF PHOTOGRAPHY

According to the article, the British Medical Association's archives contained the description of an extreme case of silver poisoning: in the 1930's there was a photographic lab assistant in Manchester whose body had absorbed so much silver in the course of a lengthy professional life that he had become a kind of photographic plate, which was apparent in the fact (as Ferber solemnly informed me) that the man's face and hands turned blue in strong light, or, as one might say, developed.

—W.G. SEBALD, *The Emigrants*

The Beauty of an Object Lies in The Beautiful Heart.

—TOUR BROCHURE, INDONESIA

CATCH LIGHT

ONE

Once, white paint was thrown out across the city, from the roofs of apartment buildings and the tops of trees for some festival, and it looked a bit like this, like nobody could get a hold of it; the paint had even come off on the hands of the people walking and they said, look, holding up a palm, this is a tree, this is a window, this is the sky.

LIGHT MATTERS

Memory is in light. It is often the most

        crystalline thing. An untuned   shift,

there where your hair was struck and above your skull

caught the light resting

        it spun blonde weather.

It gets in everywhere.

        I was once told never to place a desk by a window.

And when I did,

the window came in and all I could remember.

The intensity of light emitted should be at least 10,000 lux.

And just near enough

to bathe in it

an elbow, a little reaching the face, while you wait

in front of the device, maybe two to three feet away, or you could sit

next to a window all day, press your face to the glare, or right as

night comes on

lay your head on a light box and sleep. One girl I know

made shadow puppets in front of a projector all winter

of the birds coming back, slept

silhouetted against the screen, fingers splaying into trees.

In the back seat of a car

     in moving along

       a long road   borders

an uncut forest   a child has no word for lambent

sees each tree   blocking its own bit of sun. Raises her hand

     to the window

making shade and letting it fall away. There are certain things you

     shouldn't do like look

long enough at the sun that it begins to sear.

It's the trees at least

its very fast flickering projector.

Light where there shouldn't be light. And then you're blind. A person

    walks past and a face is almost seen but for the sun in it and yours.
    An eye rests out of light but in memory of it. And you turn but still

        the face escapes into
its shadow, its profile, backed by heavy sun it's sharp
        to look at.

The letter came back
but the words had been erased.

The memory was hinged on

        light matters. *The way it hit your face*

made me think of instances

in cinema.   And the hands only cover the eyes in shielding,

in disbelief. Seeing is believing, you look and look.

              In the eye

      the shadow loosens and when the sun gets in it's like

      the whole world goes white.

But Borges said more like blue, everything blue, went blind

just as he became custodian of 800,000 books.

Which made impeccable sense (to him).

The thing with flying is

                you're above light and night

comes on before you even see it. Who knew clouds

could throw such opaque shadow.

A girl makes an eclipse box and after the eclipse she

                      still takes it everywhere. Obliquely seen or not

at all. Night following you like

a falling trail.

      She also kept an x-ray of her lungs taken at immigration

      to use as shade on the plane.

      Marked *lungs O.K., heart in the right place.*

Here where light goes

        illegible. The refrain is a window—

film striped with it. As the camera reframes its fiction,

a face. Holding it there toward the sun. On it, a sun, shard, a white building

asserts its center. Rows and rows. The line of road

continues.   There's so much white that it might

explode the eye. There's so much white that it might

        leave the picture unfilled, its solid air shivering.

You say you're afraid of unlit rooms. Still, you cover
 your eyes in the dark, for fear of unexpected illuminations.

The first lightbulbs were all filament, all throughout the room the light
went until we'd never noticed it this large. And then a glass lip, then an
urn. A shade resembling a hat. The world showing its negative. Held to
the light disappears or becomes more distinct.

No one would take down the lightning rod on the old house.

They'd stand next to it for hours. Now we have filaments

that respond to the gentlest turn. You smash out the glass

just to touch it. A slight tingling sensation, imagined or not.

The window on the plane remains

unshuttered. Light stalks in   in beams and dusty from the

       density of air. A child

the row over draws pictures

         made of sky. She remembers hearing that sleeping under

         the sun is forbidden but under the full moon

         it's impossible. A pencil is a cloud,

         wind is a window, a child is an opaque thing.

All conduits of light retain a sheen. Magnifying glass, eclipse
box, flashlight.

   The dust of prior luminosity or a trust in the result
   of a lightbulb.

   Something when you come home and flick the switch
   and see the room all at once, a little pop, the dark going out.

Picking up the envelope, you can almost
see through it. A little light
gets in everywhere. A child puts
a hand to a flashlight and it
glows blood. It is not opaque—the hand—it is not impervious
to a beam. The density of light is a lumen, the density of a hand
is a lantern.

OPTICAL TOYS

OBSERVATORY

It begins as an attempt to untangle light. In some cities there were, still are, room-sized camera obscuras, the world comes in flipped and intact. In this case the pictures move. The heart of the blue whale is as big as a room. You could stand up in it suddenly; you could stay. Like in India inside the clock that is big enough to wander through. But the light there doesn't change; the guard tells you to go. Like the viewing machines on the shore that only last for a quarter, so gone and soon. The audible departure, a brief persistence of vision. One sun less, some measure, some minute. In a heart where it's dark and unwindowed, and sounds like this, and this, and this.

TELEIDOSCOPE

Say sun, say feather, say here. The whole
world is synonyms. Sea glass

                    from the color grass a set
              of skew mirrors—a hand hinge
        turn gently, not unlike
intense speed lifting the ground from itself

             the eye to its moving window. Where you always
see a tree or snow fenced in
by falling limbs, the feathered edge

                   of full cloud rushing
              out of frame. Using the world
      as its rocks, one makes the world its toy, i.e. to point in a lens-
shape, a pond

         rushed over its lip, the sun circles itself, the snow tremble

of all white
turned, turned
and settling.

ZOETROPE

The idea is to sit still. To see a cinema in hand. When there was no word for it: wheel. Once spun, a certain speed. Fingers glance it. You have to spin it. Before this, motion meant move. You dancing in a room with red curtains. The birds fly off against the first white snow. Although out the corner of your eye, the papers shifting. She had flipped through the pictures once and watched the diver go. Finally we are seeing ourselves doing something. It will not break or fall away. You have to keep it spinning. A whole herd of horses, or one.

KALEIDOSCOPE

From the roots of lovely & scape. From the root of when

I look small halos. From sun accumulates. From the first

letter in the Greek alphabet resembling a turn. From turning.

From bright as if lit by a stone. From bloodstone. And gem &

jet. From a letter that begins with O. From a letter that arrived

its envelope torn. From a line that could be an ampersand or

fingers forming a gesture. From the line parts left inside the envelope.

From one. From a line that resembles O. From a letter reads. *This time*

from a field. From *a slightly battered sea.*

STUTTERSIGHT

An unwound world seeks its berm. The fine edge of sight, almost but not quite fluid. A man holds up his hands a little apart and says look here. Whole worlds are folded in breast pockets, pocket watch, thaumatrope. On a string between, pulled taut, it spins. What cannot be proven in time (blink, you're still, trust me) is the fact of a toy. Here is a man who lost his hair. Here is a homeless toupee. Here is an ocean without its heart. A body without its sky. The world trues itself. Watch, he says. Here is a beginning without an end and even though you'd like to, you can't see it any other way.

CAPTIONS

The hand writes a name on the river. What the river cannot hold:

    but it is holding light, holding

        the tremor of a fingertip, loose and moving. There is a woman

who writes this same name on the river every morning.

Her god lives in the river and this prayer, a kind

of touch disturbs

           in the photograph once

you're told it's a name, you read it, you can read the water now

finger trailing ink and continuing   follows

the hand.

The geometry of a sky pinned up and still. Birds alighted on a line in simple intersections. I for one always end up losing count.

Back there, the world goes on for miles but it's too far off to make much impression. In front is a road. A landscape moves always underneath other horizons. And a slight blur in the background, a bird you didn't even notice taking off.

The face was light-erased. The city remained behind the trees. And a road that could be any other road, unnamed and straight, gone on out of frame. The swimmer pulls himself from the pond and brushes off bits of light. If the hand rests exactly on the surface of the lake. If the face looks back toward the city. It's a road you see before anything else.

A man went walking across this field years ago and still he disappears down the horizon with a machine that clicks off every mile. A storm permanently poised on the edge of the field, made of cloud and settling sun. Here the face is shorn with sky.

Someone passes a picture window and sees the face clearly for a split second but still after it is down the road out of sight what is that seeing called.

Weather is abstract until it touches the skin. There is talk of snow beginning, of that instant that has never been captured on film.

FIVE EYES

1

Look away: beat a quick retreat into

the blank back of an eyelid. I had a doll whose eyes were always

open so I thought she was always awake. A hundred years ago

there were doctors running around with bags of glass

eyes in every possible iris. Just in case. Even when there's nothing to see

we'd still like the possibility of seeing it.

Clap your hands three times and you will wake up

with a glass eye in your hand.

2

Migratory animals find their way by a sense of direction and the weather.
We say the air is thinner but don't reach up to spool it. And ghosting a cloud
is another inside

       based on a fold. The weather-eye went moonblind.
       In the snow you can track anything except white.
       Another lid in its orbit air. Placed directly to the eye,
       the eye can be measured by a system of scales. A twenty-
       step staircase. A whole sentence stretches out overhead
       and you recite it because you know how. This is
       how you learned. While the habitat here sometimes teems
       we are sorry, closed, etc. The through in it reaches past the
       sentence.   Do you even know what you're seeing

3

The most common eye color is brown. But upon closer inspection, you said,
I see streaks of green and gold. If only to have a tiger-eye. Darwin wrote
the Indian elephants in the London zoo shed he said *abundant tears in situations*
of pain and sorrow. Sadly,
there has been much evidence to disprove this. The only
emotional animal, we shelter our eyes in intense sun and weep over onions.

4

The eye is subject to none of the
shape inconsistencies of noses and ears. It's always
round in proportion. In fact if you cut it open
a whole world would roll out, intact. Darwin's
only instrument was his eyes. Should we bother
drawing pictures of light?

5

To eye. A change in weather or the quality of a painted-on iris. As it comes
closer it is less distinct.
Skin, water, the sun overhead until you can't look at it. Letters
              read into a sea. In low or intense light
              all detail is lost in perceiving the sheer. Light travels and picks up
every particle on the way and illuminates it. You see the air moving, like that.
There must be distance, he said,
for the thing to be seen. So I hold you out from me and say now—
let me look at you.

CLOUD & BULB

OCCLUSION

It begins *it started* because it always begins without
an actual point of origin and suddenly a constellation is replaced so rightly
> with falling rain. Finally someone sees it's all repeating,
> feeding back into a place
where it's dark enough that it's easy to believe
you're alone but you know you're not (you saw the others come in behind
> you) and moving

quietly among these looping sounds that remain indistinct—like not-laugh-
> ing—but familiar

like the beginning of a laugh—that air
intake that pause that is hot and not at all empty that pause and
again the images are changing in color now—rain has a little color to it—
> and a face is imposed

lightly on a room, it is always this way, an uneasy eye at the corner of the image
blinks quickly meaning How did I end up here because of course

eyes have their own way of saying good-bye, or saying
this is not the right room

A SALGADO PHOTOGRAPH

The toys the children are playing with are actually bones.
And the horses among them are real.
Light glints off the dry white
in a doorway
lets the sun in. Move
to play the bones closer.
You are crossing the land of the dead now,
its shadows and paths. Bones make the map.
You had never seen faces on a child like that.

PROFILE FOR A FACE IN PASSING

Compendium: the bird is in the eyeball. Reflected.
Contains its

        only chance   at flight.   Many ways of saying:
this is the last look from the last face on earth
     imagine slipping it off
     imagine there is something more   intrinsic than the eyes,
                                 their luminous spoor.

SOUND FOR A CERTAIN LANDSCAPE

In the next dream your eyes will be open. What it should sound like—
the night and its quiet new after dark. A place you remember but have
never been. White sails, or snow. When I count to ten you will wake up
—breath in a bell jar calm. A photograph of blankness, look long
enough and there's slight life. The horizon handmade, one black bird
empties the sky. When I count to ten you will awake in an unfamiliar
place. When I count the sound of ten.

Where the lightbulb bursts the whole world
drips undefined. Effaced in its own motion
and ultra-light. Too much of a good thing
and there's a carnival ride shaped like a wheel
that never stops to let the riders off.
Someone thought enough to bring a camera
so all of this spinning wouldn't be lost.
What I really wanted was to stay up here
for a while and get a good look at the spectators.
When we finally slow down, hold my hand, they seated us
like this, said: *Make sure the other doesn't get left.*
The stars are flung up there. They burst and turn.

A photographer sets out to document clouds.
A traceable inclination to stop anything in motion
and hold it up for better viewing. X-ray, eclipse
box, light comes through leaf too. The sky a series
of rooms.

Here the photographer divorces horizon
from sky. Intent upon movement scat-
tered from its surface. The last compass
up here lost its way in an overwhelmed
hand. And the clouds seem to be split-
ting from within, tearing along thin
seams of sun.

In this version the eye must stay closed for an exact

duration. The eye as opposed

to a shutter. When the eye opens it will notice something

different. Has the eye burned this into remembrance

as a camera would? You have ten seconds to recount everything

that will change in this room.

The sun chooses to render its window
impotent. So the last birds leaving the plaza are
unseen. The sun haunts closed eyes—games she
played as a child, imagining the sun would burn
away her eye but then someone would
lick her wounds and the sun would be gone.

The blur is the world. Line wet against a window. A trusted transparency slightly erased. When the form is familiar but the blur gets inside. A language you've never learned comes from another room. The way ladders lead to the bodies gone across them and windows to a former face. If this weather doesn't let up. A lamppost unlit, documented in more sheen. Water on glass in the unstrung sun, metallic wash, reflection from inside. The photographer's hand is even more the ghost. If this weather, this winter, this window.

FINALLY A PHOTOGRAPH

We equate water and light.

Each hand has its own tremble. The tenor of reaching out yields
a brief trailing gleam, a minimal disturbance of course:
water shivers when touched. Or from within.

>One bird in a big sky is slowly wielding its arc.
>We cannot drown in the sun

Water lies on its landscape, where

>light doesn't travel
>sound doesn't travel

sound never dissipates when you're speaking in the dark
(speaking is one way of drowning).

Handwriting conforms to methods induced by time
the wrist precedes the fingers
the whole body shivers
at once or not at all

Skin is memory: A window once shattered and was no longer
a window. The face you showed me was
not your own.

A person walks by you in the other direction
haunts your next steps—

we stopped telling ghost stories years ago.

Because what follows is not always sequential—astray:
photographs are choices.

Some days the sky is fallen,

softly,

among other things.

Some days it stays pinned.

You will notice the sky falling
in this photograph.

The color white was

                              an instance of landscape aberration

                              a chance to be your own

     illuminated

     cutout

     from the world's edge.

Motion: a bird hurls into the sky.

Emits a little light. Its crescendoing tendencies:

A million tiny teeth.

of light.

A tree is on fire

but still no one comes

in from the rain

A MANUAL OF PHOTOGRAPHY

CHAPTER 1: AN OVERVIEW

The window was more obvious than the camera. Vocal ghosts made explicit in lens and call. Although this goes without saying, images must be fixed, before they come to light. Whole histories of keep. Emulsion, albumen, and water. There will be paper, and shadows, and a heart traced where the body would lie. There will break open. What is not here, haunt, if I remember, you are a saint in the sun my windowpane.

CHAPTER 2: THE CAMERA BODY

A certain amount of light passes through the camera body. It touches the whole face at once. And the eye, the lens, everything else. Picture a ghost in a white room, that potential. Held us to the wall, stay we say but the going. Bodies between hands and stilled, sill. The photograph allowed us to imagine our insides better, such a flimsy skin now not of paint or flesh. A heart beating there, or it did.

CHAPTER 3: THE CAMERA LENS

Always this is happening in a field, it is dusk, open mouth to an invasive sky. A photograph is afterlife. Images do not stick to windows. Light must be bent, to return, come back. We think burn, etch, ingrain. Imagine a sear and a sound imperceptible but still. The sound it takes to stay. First there is the equivalence of light to time, and light to brands on your arm an image. Fractions of seconds for shadow, more for detail in the lights, one for sun blown out. Here gone equals one, a photograph emerging of pure white.

CHAPTER 4: THE SHUTTER

The tense of a muscle or the first time a running horse is frozen, all the legs lifted. The lid of an eye is timed, leaves opening, a levee and a window, curtains thrown back, the water comes in, it is hard to leave a window so bare, so wide, things still make it in past the glass and settle in here, shift and shadow and stay. The shutter blinds the eye behind it, glare, lens flaring. Close the curtains, you say, as the parade passes by.

CHAPTER 5: FILM EXPOSURE

If you can imagine a system based on the subtlest of difference. A test, the surface of a shell. Where the light pools, or pulling the dark. If you had found an hour and watched it. Which bears repeating: the exact moment of a photograph is never exactly again. Dead like a second, build-up and brink. Sun-sought in a sea, in a turning cheek. Consider: in the face of sky-glare, heavy snow and sand, given more light, they white, and the dark mane, holding back it blacks in.

CHAPTER 6: THE NEGATIVE

A sky as opposed to its cloud, eye to its iris, inverse ghost. On a thin strip emulates, the fruit of that tree showed up all white. But it wasn't. In some cultures, photographs are terrifying things.

CHAPTER 7: THE PRINT

A room without windows is essential. And a radio for sound other than light coming out, imagine it, how you can't help but hear now that the room is so still given to whisper. And you turn the music down every now and then to confirm it. The photograph coming up from the chemical, a face, a fiction, all of us now still in our skin. Hello, I've been looking for you. Most photographers will tell you, emerging with a newly fixed photograph—I am now unaccustomed to the light.

CHAPTER 8: THE LIGHT METER

One photographer always read his wrong, believed the world to be darker and so underexposed it that way. The people became dark imprints of a human looking form, looking lost on the land, which therefore, though dark, is imprinted with spots of brightest white, blown out, nothing there except the door.

CHAPTER 9: PRESENTATION

The spot on the photograph where the eye lingers. Must have caught a glare, a glass, a new ring. A curiously blind sun in the face. A photograph is the past so dearly. Even now in your hands. *I think it does hurt, a little, to be photographed.* I think it does sting a bit in the sun. It must. Hold it, hold still, says the photographer. You could place your hands on it, but never around.

APPENDIX A: BEGINNINGS OR THE HISTORY OF PHOTOGRAPHY

The eyes are the last to go. In the photograph the dead mingle among dripping trees and incandescent weather. There is no hint of what's to come. A photograph cannot, in itself, divine. In some cultures any power so great without a voice is suspect. So the photographer was split, his camera handled as a curse. Too great to be destroyed, so buried in the field. When we go there now and hear nothing at all. We handle the old photos by their edges. We whistle softly at the ghosts.

NOTES

"Occlusion" was inspired by Leighton Pierce's installation *Warm Occlusion,* which I sat in for hours, in the North Gallery of the University of Iowa's Museum of Art in 2006. The titles of the poems in "A Manual of Photography" were inspired by *Black and White Photography: A Basic Manual,* by Henry Horenstein. The quote in "Chapter 9: Presentation" is from Diane Arbus.

COLOPHON

Catch Light was designed at Coffee House Press,
in the historic Grain Belt Brewery's Bottling House near downtown Minneapolis.
The text is set in Garamond.

FUNDER ACKNOWLEDGMENTS

Coffee House Press is an independent nonprofit literary publisher. Our books are made possible through the generous support of grants and gifts from many foundations, corporate giving programs, state and federal support, and through donations from individuals who believe in the transformational power of literature. This book received special support from the National Poetry Series. Coffee House receives major general operating support from the McKnight Foundation, the Bush Foundation, from Target, and from the Minnesota State Arts Board, through an appropriation by the Minnesota State Legislature and from the National Endowment for the Arts. Coffee House also receives support from: three anonymous donors; Abraham Associates; the Elmer L. and Eleanor J. Andersen Foundation; Allan Appel; Bill Berkson; the James L. and Nancy J. Bildner Foundation; the Patrick and Aimee Butler Family Foundation; the Buuck Family Foundation; the law firm of Fredrikson & Byron, PA.; Jennifer Haugh; Anselm Hollo and Jane Dalrymple-Hollo; Jeffrey Hom; Stephen and Isabel Keating; Robert and Margaret Kinney; the Kenneth Koch Literary Estate; Allan & Cinda Kornblum; Seymour Kornblum and Gerry Lauter; the Lenfestey Family Foundation; Ethan J. Litman; Mary McDermid; Rebecca Rand; Debby Reynolds; the law firm of Schwegman, Lundberg, Woessner, PA.; Charles Steffey and Suzannah Martin; John Sjoberg; Jeffrey Sugerman; Stu Wilson and Mel Barker; the Archie D. & Bertha H. Walker Foundation; the Woessner Freeman Family Foundation; and many other generous individual donors.

NATIONAL ENDOWMENT FOR THE ARTS

This activity is made possible in part by a grant from the Minnesota State Arts Board, through an appropriation by the Minnesota State Legislature and a grant from the National Endowment for the Arts. MINNESOTA STATE ARTS BOARD

TARGET.

To you and our many readers across the country,
we send our thanks for your continuing support.

Good books are brewing at www.coffeehousepress.org